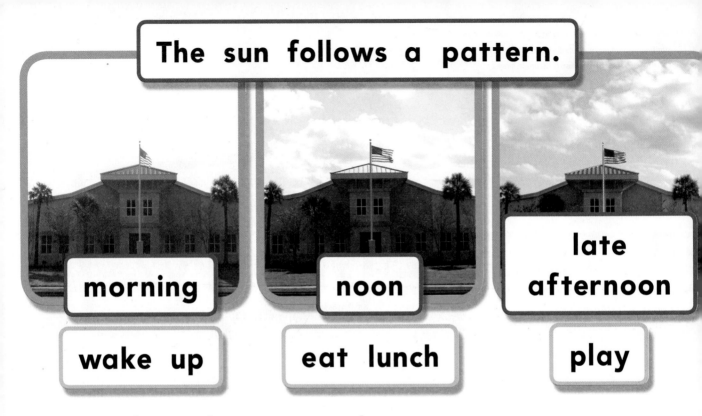

The sun follows a pattern.

morning

wake up

noon

eat lunch

late afternoon

play

It is day when we wake up.

What patterns happen every day?

The moon comes out.

The sun goes down.

It is night when we go to bed.

moon

clouds

sun

We can see the sun and clouds.

What can we see in the sky during the day?

big

small

close

far

Things that are close look big.
Things that are far away look small.

stars

moon

We can see the moon and stars.

What can we see in the night sky?

clouds

We sometimes see clouds.

Identify the Day and Night Pattern

Have children act out the pattern of day and night. For example, you may have a group of three children with one being the sun, one being the moon, and one being himself or herself. The sun moves across the sky to represent morning, noon, and late afternoon. The child does activities appropriate for each time. Then the sun sets and the moon is visible. The child acts out going to bed. Make sure to have the pattern repeat.

Draw the Sky

Ask children to look at the sky. Remind them not to look directly at the sun. Then have children draw the day sky that they saw. Ask partners to take turns describing what they saw. Encourage children to view the night sky at home. Have them draw a picture of the night sky and share it with the rest of the class.

Vocabulary	
clouds	stars
moon	sun
sky	